Praise for Allen Morris Jones

For *Last Year's River*

"Allen Jones's book is full of strengths, not least of which is its furious readability."

—Thomas McGuane

"Allen Jones knows the West by heart."

—William Kittredge

"The quiet space in which his characters . . . reside is what carves out a niche for this book that has formerly been occupied only by true literary greats."

—Barnes & Noble
Discover Great New Writers Citation

For *A Bloom of Bones*

"Jones's novel seems to have emerged from an older, more elemental world, a mythic, almost biblical place..."

—*Library Journal*

"An exquisitely crafted book, and one to be savored."

—*Foreword Magazine*

For *Sweeney on the Rocks*

"Think 'Goodfellas' with a screenplay by Donald E. Westlake, set in the landscape of 'A River Runs through It'."

—*Booklist*

"A terrific, stylish writer . . ."

—*Kirkus Reviews*

Mumblecusser
and other poems

Mumblecusser
and other poems

First edition in hardcover originally published by
the Drumlummon Institute, Helena, Montana.

Cover painting, "Two Buttes at Dawn," by Dale Livezey
Cover Design and Text Design by Allen Morris Jones

Manufactured in the United States of America

ISBN 13: 978-0-9961560-5-9

Published in the United States by

Bangtail Press
P. O. Box 11262
Bozeman, MT 59719
www.bangtailpress.com

For Corey and Karen

Table of Contents

Mumblecusser
and other poems

I'm mostly talking to myself, of course.
Like the nine-fingered man who keeps saying,
"Careful how you light that firecracker."

Note to Self

You are salt water, mostly; you are electricity,
dancing. You are an inexplicable eruption
of awareness in a void. Your brain, 2 percent
of your body mass, accounts for 20 percent of
your calorie burn. You retain your fingerprints,
although the skin is replaced every 27 days.
Bowel to belly to tongue, you are host to 5 pounds
of bacteria. A species of mite on your scalp
is distinct from a species of mite on your nose.
Spouses, over time, come to carry each other's biota.
Genetically, we are summations of our dead.
You are a delivery mechanism for your genes.
The dead may offer commentary but it will tilt
toward sarcasm. You will be carried by the living,
and sooner than you had expected. The multitude
of small kindnesses occurring in the world (now
and now) are somehow enough to counterbalance
the rare monstrosities. It's a wash. The dead tilt
toward astonishment. Intellect and reason argue
against arrogance. You are only one among 8 billion,
nothing special. And yet you are extraordinary.
The universe has never seen anything quite like you.
You are a stone under a stream of exploding stars.
You will be astonished, and sooner than you
had expected.

Hawk in a Winter Tree

More a suggestion of hawk,
a semaphore smudge of feathers,
a thumbnail smear;
the swivel of its head,
the gears,
talons tight around loose bark;
the ground at a distance
or no distance at all
for these eyes;
under the snow, a rustle,
a mouse busy in dry grass;
elsewhere, a rabbit blinks
a single black eye.
A mind one with itself
considers the field,
the farmhouse beyond;
a thread of smoke,
the muted, crumbling
catastrophe of snow
beginning to fall.
The hawk, imperious
in the bones of a winter tree,
surveys what is, or was,
or will be, while the watcher,
hunched deep in a red coat,
considers the hawk,
and considers the winter tree.

Clickbait

We are at the mercy of our animal selves;
there are in fact nine aspects of our vulnerability
to narrative and you won't believe number five.
Ten thousand years ago, poking at a campfire,
huddling close against the ominous rustle of leaves
outside the light, a grandfather whispered to a half circle
of children, wide-eyed and rapt, about the eight things
you should know to survive until tomorrow, and oh
number two will astonish. A young wife, cheeks scrubbed
against last night's tears, gave six reasons to leave.
Number four will break your heart. A rich man owes it all
to these three morning habits; a celebrity has one
simple exercise to keep her arms toned, to maintain
your envy. Click through for the trick, the secret, the key
to your messy, beautiful hardscrabble days. Your friends
from childhood, once so cherished, have disappeared
into their own lives, your parents are aging, your child
is nearly grown and gone; click here to be comforted;
click here to be understood. Click here to feel
not quite so alone. Click here to unsubscribe.

Twenty-Eight Below at 8:00 AM

He feeds out alfalfa hay alone,
cutting twine in the bed of his truck,
kicking out the flakes, climbing down
to idle a few lengths further along
then back into the bed. The cows come
to him, drawn patient and urgent.
They rely on him. The ranch truck belled in
on the doors still idles along, smooth enough.
The underworld exhaust mingles
with steam from the living bodies,
the breath and warmth from the living
drawn together into a fragile gauze.
The morning so cold and so quiet,
tires cracking at frozen, hoof-chopped mud.
In an hour or so, there will be a kitchen
and a kitchen table, coffee, boots
collapsed by the door, gloves dripping,
overalls rank; a wife, familiar; they are
familiar to each other. A hand on a shoulder,
an incidental gesture of affection
or perhaps reassurance. I am here.
The richest men in the world do not
have this: a warm kitchen after cold work,
the honest regard of another, hay
enough to feed out through the winter,
probably; a hand on a shoulder and this coffee,
warm enough. They might have everything
else, those men, but they don't have this.
This is ours.

Dinner Table Conversation

We could talk about the scars,
the day's cuts, slices, stabs, losses
that crumpled your heart
like a paper cup, small cruelties
that left you reduced and trembling;
or no, rather, how about the triumphs?
The kind words tossed your way,
quiet encouragements suspended
in a matrix of coffee mugs
and printer jams. You are well liked,
you are admired.
"How's your chicken?"
Light years away, a galaxy is exploding,
without a sound; I read a thing.
The sun is even now somewhere sinking
into the sea. For my part,
certain epiphanies keep plucking
at the same old strings.
"Can you pass the bread?"
A stranger at the gas station
seemed to know me. Damnedest thing.
He touched my shoulder. "Buddy," he said,
"you and me, it's our turn now
to grow old."

Satan at a Stoplight

He sits at the wheel, thrumming rust-red claws on
the dash, anonymous in the field of idling engines
and blooming exhaust, the acrid odors of impatience.
Reluctant tenant since his famous, humbling fall
from th'Ethereal skies, he's never felt at home here,
not really, not until he bought this souped up black Toyota,
tricked it out with spinners, lift kit, a basso beat
deep enough to shake windows, a hood full
of rumbling penal fire. Home. He can hardly believe his luck.
The soul of Henry Ford, tangled in a rosary, dangles
from his rear view. He adores the five-lane freeways
where he can drive with his left blinker always on, swerve
and slow unpredictably, eat fast food, talk to his agent
on a cell phone, wink at the Mormon family of four
as he cuts them off close, testing Dad's capacity
for the profane. He adores the cloverleafs, the exhilarating
rev toward takeoff before a squealing stop, inches
from a bumper sticker. "It's a life, not a choice."
He gives them a horny thumbs up, grinning around
his mouthful of razor blades. But most of all,
it occurs to him now, watching the swaggering pod
of slow pedestrians in the crosswalk, the teenagers
losing their jeans and hip young mothers with strollers,
and phones, most of all he loves the noise, the diesel engines
clattering like coins in a can, the angry horns
and wailing ambulances, the eternal cacophony
of car alarms and construction. He bows his head
to fiddle with the radio, delighted by how we've all
finally forgotten that indeed God speaks, but only
in silence.

Kindergarten Colors

I was taught, incidental
to a larger lesson, that light
creates color. In darkness,
every object defaults to black.
Funny how the mind works.
Forty-seven years later I still
remember a scraped elbow,
and how it came to me
as a revelation that my blood
had only been biding its time,
colorless until light could offer it
a nice rusty red. We are vaults
of unrevealed color, it seems.
We are cathedrals glowing
from within. We are all miracles
in hiding, waiting patiently
for good attention to be paid.
We are all waiting for attention
to be paid.

Father and Son

Hearing the words or
seeing them on the page,
I was always the son, the
apprentice and private.
Until you, in my arms,
twisting tic-tac toes
against my belt, digging
for purchase, made me the
father. And this is only
the start

of my gratitude.

Window Seat

One of the few consolations of aging, it seems,
is the view it offers, the privileged glimpse of
irrigation circles as from above. Sore knees,
an unstable gut, twitchy memory, but (flip side)
you are given this front row seat to the big picture.
Turns out, we've been at the mercy of our animal
selves all this time. Each generation keeps
painting its own silhouette inside a template
cut by biology. War, and everything else.
We are social creatures. Traveling from void
to void, we need the esteem of others the way
we need kidneys, a liver. Young men will kill
and die, kill and die, and only for acceptance.
Seeing that, maybe it's wisdom. I don't know.
What I do know, I filled a bird feeder
this morning like any number of other aging men
in America, feeling only that it was somehow
the right thing to do. This modest gift offered
to nameless brown fluttering jewels, wrens
or something else. Released from certain urgencies,
I appreciate the morning reminder, over coffee,
that we are not so alone after all. This reminder,
the pleasures of it, seems baked into my biology.
I dig it, despite the white commas of bird shit
now streaking my nice brown fence.

We Are Water

We will live with
our outrage the way
a river lives with
its rocks, shaping
and being shaped.
You are water, my love;
you are water to me,
quiet and patient and strong.
And cutting, over time,
through every smug
motherfucking cliff.

Distracted by Work

Nike hat worn backwards, the boy stood under
the basketball hoop and lifted one leg high
to dribble the ball underneath. He glanced my way
to see if I'd caught his trick. Playing Simon Says
on the trampoline, he said, "Tell me to do that
butt-bounce thing again, Dadda." I'm forty-seven.
The boy is six. I worry about this. In the backyard
with his mother, he kicked dirt obliquely our way,
then glanced at us. He might as well have been
shaking my shirt. Pay *attention* to me. These
are the days when he was learning to read,
when he could go to the couch with a comic
and be lost. Then: "Dadda, do you want to go play
Legos with me?" Alone for too long, he tries
out his portfolio of sound effects. The *pkchews*
of laser beams, *brrrrupps* of engines revving, bullets
pinging off into the distance. You break my heart, boy.
The years are coming, of course, when you won't
care to play basketball, when the Legos will sit
in dust-covered bins in the basement, when the stream
of sounds from your lips will go sullenly silent.
I should have more time, then.

Dog Stars

Like you, I have a hard time with constellations.
Not just the frustrating, connect-the-dots nonsense
of imagined shapes but the assumption that certain stories
will help make sense of the infinite. Why those stories
and not some others? Why not *our* stories, is my thought.
Not Leo up there but Henry, my old black Lab,
ears cocked forward puzzling his way through a command.
Dead now fourteen years, that's Henry up there for sure.
I'm staking a claim. And why let the Pleiades keep
rolling around unchallenged when there's my grandfather
with his four fingers, one of them lost to a cane grinder
when he was a child? Instead of Ursus minor and major
why not that mule deer buck I killed in 1982
with its perfect, star-shaped antlers? This is not,
as the Chinese would tell you, the year of the rat,
the cat, or the dragon. Rather, it's the year
of mortgage payments and construction paper,
crayons and glue sticks. It's the year of Costco mums
on the porch and Covid masks, maybe a new tennis racket.
Arguments on Facebook, friends won and lost.
It's the year of standing in the backyard waiting
for the dog to pee. Staring up at the emerging stars
and thinking helplessly, again and again, they go on forever.
They just go on forever.

Jump Shooting, 1986

Teenagers, we used to jump shoot the Yellowstone.
That was us on the shoulder of Highway 89, glassing
the river. If we spotted birds, we'd knock on the nearest door:
"Mind if we cut through your pasture?" Or maybe we'd just
scurry across, road to river. No one seemed to mind much,
local kids in camouflage and waders, hunching through
the willows to rise, shotguns snug to shoulders, the geese
below us. Then the whir of wings, honking, and one, two, three
shots each. A shattering of the frozen morning. If we were lucky,
a goose angling down to tremble on the rocks, wings askew.
Joy isn't the word here but it's close. Joy and loss.

Years passed.

If you live in Montana long enough, you will eventually
come to remark upon its decline. That's what I really want
to write about. How we all manage to mourn for the time
before. That was my childhood. These days, though,
if you stand above Paradise Valley at night, the dark floor is
carpeted in yard lights and the river grows little on its banks
so well as knapweed and no trespassing signs. The station
keeps backing away from the train. Honestly, it's probably
better not to pay too much attention. You're only going to have
your heart broken, again and again. If not now then soon.
It just takes time. Just a little more time.

Tuesday Morning Sermon

We'll get started as soon as the rest arrive
Thank you for coming, thank you, yes, thank you.
There's more chairs there in the hallway.
Okay, good. You probably heard the rumors.
They're true, more or less. I spoke to God,
and just yesterday. He said to say hello.
You all should get more rest, he said. You're looking tired.
And for Christ's sake, don't be so hard on yourselves.
You're only human, and that's his fault.
About disappointment. Career, family, friends.
You might want to look first at your expectations.
We're all struggling, he said. Can you hear me
in the back? Okay, thanks. You've been spending
your mornings in dialogue with certain regrets
and grievances, gnawing around that familiar gristle.
A question: When will you be done? Remember
that your life has days the way a wall has bricks.
Tomorrow is a tossup. On the beach, a wave
is already rolling that will, when it breaks, catch
the light just so, illuminating the bait fish suspended
in its belly. In the brush beside the Yellowstone River,
a whitetail fawn nudges its mother for milk.
They stand together, dappled in cottonwood light,
hidden from every other living thing. God said
pay attention. You should take what you can get,
spirit wise. You've got your breaking wave,
you've got your fawn. Otherwise, it's iffy.
Questions so far?

Throwing Rocks on the Gallatin

Consider the carpet
of them, the infinite floor,
the array of red,

blue, green stones, spread smooth
down the course of the river.
Infinite. But yours,

son, oh yours was the
only one to make such a
fine and pleasant plop

as it found its place.

Tiny Triumphs

The fried egg yolk stayed
splendidly intact, shimmering,
despite how I'd cracked it too high
above the pan; my shirt matched
my pants without a plan and the coffee
tasted so good, bitter and rich.
My wife waved me to a stop as I left,
opening the truck door to kiss
me goodbye. The light stayed green
just long enough, and the next song
in the shuffle recalled old friends.
The world wobbles alarmingly
and the news sells tickets to tragedy
but there's a woman who cares
for me and a child who needs me,
and just now, sitting at my desk,
I have this moment, this improbable
moment. Awareness slops out
over the rim. It's not only that I am here,
alive and loved, it's that I am allowed,
for some reason,
to know it.

Halloween Candy

Watching my son sit cross-legged on the floor,
sorting through his bag, upending the bag
to move all the gummy bears into one pile,
Kit Kats into another, oversized Tootsie Rolls,
Almond Joys. Such richness, such absurd wealth,
such a sense of order imposed before the slaughter,
the satisfying rip and tear and chew, the miracle
of each bar lost among the abundance.
One more Nerds, just another Snickers.
By the end of November, there will remain
a small bag of m&ms. A single bag to be saved,
treasured, considered. He might eat it one day.
Such a perfect little package. It reminds me now
of driving through Oakland a few years ago,
five lanes of stop-and-go traffic, the muted cacophony
of engines and horns, the odors of exhaust
and seared ozone. Mozart on the radio couldn't
drown out five lanes of despair. I sat behind
the wheel reduced, diminished, lost within
the horde. There are so many of us now.
There are so goddamn many of us.

The River

There's a boy on the corner who sells
anything you might need, door hinges
to shoe laces, belt buckles to wooden matches.
Last month, I bought a river from him.
"How much is that?" I asked, pointing
to the river. I won't tell you what I paid,
embarrassed that you might think I took
advantage. But we shook on it, and I brought
the river home, showing it to a blanket
in the corner. "Do you know any tricks?"
I asked, trying to pet it. But it kept twisting
away. The boy had said it could speak
but had neglected to mention the language.
It babbled endlessly, loudest at night.
No one slept. Early mornings, late evenings,
if I had the house to myself, I would sit with it.
My wife finally took me aside. "I know
you're fond of the river, but this can't go on."
I made a case for one more day. "I'm picking up
a few words," I said. "I'm *this* close."
She seemed skeptical. "One more day?"
I nodded, and kissed her, and wept
helplessly down her dry cheek.

Going For Optimism

We're not so old. Your childhood
just as close as mine, no further than
our last game of hide and seek. Remember
how your body responded to that spot
under the porch? Shaded, cool, the packed dirt
smelling like cobwebs and mice, wet dogs,
the hush of it, the pleasure of eavesdropping
on the others as they rummaged about outside,
lifting branches, pouncing behind sheds,
those kids who were *it,* the predators;
forts made from pillows held a similar appeal.
Resentment and fear, I'm afraid, are defaults,
not unlike how illiteracy is a default. Friends,
it's goddamned hard learning to read;
just as hard to see the world through eyes
not your own. Empathy is a motherfucker.
You want some good news? The story
of America is the story of our hearts
unclenching, gradually, painfully, needles
in the skin, turning pages that resist
being turned but turning them nonetheless,
a small hand reaching into the gloom
to swat at the toe of a sneaker. "Gotchyou!"
Urging us to roll out, one by one, blinking,
draped in cobwebs and leaves, to squint
at the silhouette above us. A friend, surely,
but strange to us now, alien, wreathed as she is
in such a dazzling, unexpected light.

Billionaires

"You got your two kinds of people
in the world," he said. "You got those
who buy your scratch offs, your Powerballs,
then you got your other kind. My people
are the dreamers, is what I'm saying.
The hopers. I walk into a party, I look
for an eager swivel, a bright look.
Buddy, not for me the smug, the arrogant,
the satisfied with what they got.
Those guys can go fuck themselves.
But hey, listen: What they don't want
you to know? To dream is to briefly
possess the dream. We're all billionaires
buddy, if you think about it. At least until
they announce the numbers."

Keats Wrote His Name In Water

I have my ideas about what it means
to live a decent and good life; I'll assume
some overlap with the rest of the world
but the outside edges, the filament fringes,
are mine. I'll fill you in later. Our new puppy
tilts her nose to the ghost of anyone
who just left the room; songbirds fly through
an infrared world broken into private estate
by song, the drabbest of them glowing neon green.
I saw a thing on TV. There's a species of vole,
I've read, uniquely wired to recognize a prophet
and yet still it prefers the wisdom it finds
underground, nosing through roots. I had
a dream with all the answers I might ever need.
By the time I poured oatmeal into boiling water
it had faded, leaving only a soapy residue
of despair. I stood bereft above the steam.
Hey, listen: You do what you can and then
you're done. Certain notions sting. Me?
I was the guy who held his ear to a beehive,
hoping only to hear the ocean.

The Gallery

The boy's masterpieces, when he deigns to show them
to us, come as crumpled accordions from the basement
of his backpack, worthless until illuminated by the lamps
of the living room, displaced from kindergarten toward
our amazement. "You did this? How wonderful!" I study
his little face, a stranger to subterfuge, and watch it reappraise,
reevaluate, reconsider, shift on the fly to self-satisfaction.
He's a genius and wasn't even aware. We keep them around,
the march of stick figures with catenary smiles, the acres of jade
green grass under frozen yellow suns, sheafs of perfectly square
houses, chimneys crowned by gray curlicues. His mother
takes the latest scribble and smooths it flat, fixes it to the fridge
with magnets. I pour a glass of cheap Malbec from the box
and throw on an expression of polite interest, browsing couch
to credenza. "I see a little Rothko in this one," I say. Pathos
in a flying bird, a squashed letter M. "Maybe this one symbolizes
our mortality." To which she responds, "Don't be such a dick."
Which isn't what I'm going for here, not at all. Wife, can't you
see my uncertainty? My fear at what comes next? There are days
when I feel myself crumpling. When our house tilts and twists
at its perfect corners, when my smile fails to reach the dots
of my eyes and the wax sun chars the edges of its page. I study
this idyll, our family holding hands, and we look so alone. Wife,
there are days when it's all I can do to keep it inside the lines.
Wife, there are days when I am simply terrified.

Different Kinds of Happiness

Seventeen years old, going skiing with my friends,
anticipating the day ahead, a station wagon
with a half tank of gas and AC/DC at tribal volume,
maybe a pint of Beam going around—we were so young,
so gloriously young, so unified in our swagger.
It was us against the world, man. And goddamn, what joy.
Maybe I'd never feel it again. I knew even then
that I would never feel it again. Thirty years later, though,
driving up to the hill with my boy, from a car seat
in the back, I heard, "Dadda, can you put on the rock star
music?" We then sang together about all those dirty deeds
done so dirt cheap. And can I tell you how happy I was?
Just so easily, I was nothing but joy. There was nowhere
else in the world that I wanted to be—nowhere but
going skiing with my boy.

Saturday Morning, 1979

Told to help in my grandmother's garden
I had my hoe, unwieldy in my small hands,
chopping hard, then timidly, resentfully,
as likely to cut through the potato plants
and corn, peas, squash, tomatoes, as any weeds.
Sweat bees trapped within my elbow protested
with stings while I trailed tears and destruction.
It would never be over. Never.

Yesterday evening, I sliced a tomato from
my wife's garden, crushing the stem between
my fingers. Do you know that smell? The spice
of sun and sweat and bees. And just then,
just so easily, Mary Jones, my grandmother, gone
twenty years and more, sat beside me in the shade
of her blueberry bushes. One gardener to another
she passed me a milk jug of ice water, dripping
and priceless. Forever kind

in that forever shade.

Bare Roots

My wife and I went to Costco. Christ,
we're always going to Costco. But today
we bought three fruit trees bare root,
in cardboard and sawdust; stems, really.
Just branches sticking up. A steal at $19.95.
The labels—peach, cherry, apple...I'll
assume they know what they're talking about.
Tomorrow I'll dig holes for them and press
some nice dark loamy potting soil around
the nebulae of the roots, mixing it
with the thick clay of our yard, and I'll
water them with a hose. And in fifty years,
if I'm lucky, a child not unlike my child, a
seven-year-old, will dig his bare toes into
the bark or wrap her hands around
a lower branch and swing up to find
the cherry, the peach, the apple. The passing
sweetness, and the smear of juice on their
cheeks. The satisfying spit of a seed. I won't
be around to say it then so I suppose I should
say it now: If all goes well, beautiful,
beautiful child, you're welcome.
You're so welcome.

A Consolation

There are eight billion of us
on the planet, eight billion and more.
If we all jumped at once, on the count of three,
a coordinated effort, the world might
feel it a little, I suppose, might wobble
a smidge as it turns before proceeding apace.
If we all crowded into one corner,
if we all pressed, tight as bricks,
shoulder to shoulder on the tip of a peninsula,
the axis might budge to one side, a fraction
of a degree. Otherwise, I'm not sure
we're as important as we might like to think.
The business of being alive on the skin
of this little planet is ours and ours alone.
The mistakes we're making now will be forgotten.
And that's good news, I suppose. I'm fifty
and only just now starting to figure
some of this shit out.

Coyote and Magpie

"Brother, pickings is slim these days.
roadkill's in clear decline, and the taste
has gone plum out of it. The world's
not like it was. Where we're headed,
there's little or no good news, and at such
a rapid clip; brother, let's stick together
in the face of such despair, we need
to help one, another, we need..."

Coyote lay grinning, chin on paws,
refraining from comment, until, stretching,
spreading toes, yawning, he voted his assent
and moved to adjourn, as was his wont,
with a snap and snarl, a sneeze, a cough
of glowing black and white feathers
curling soft across the dazzling and
delicious world.

Dubious Circumstances

When I die, I want it to be under dubious circumstances
A dozen cops rummaging through my apartment,
stepping long over the outline of my body, a letter
fallen from my hands (one corner soaked with blood)
and an unshaven detective chewing his dead cigar,
silver flask hidden in his pocket. Jowly, jaded, still
smelling of last night's woman, he'll glance at my outline,
at the letter, and with the dismissive confidence
that has made him so many enemies, he'll go straight
to the bookshelf, running through the spines to find
the single volume set upside down, as if in a rush.
I hope he has a taste for French poetry, or knows someone
who does, his ex-wife maybe. He's never stopped
loving her. Together, amid the slaughtered remains
of Chinese takeout, they'll sift through my marginalia.
I can see her curled on the couch with her shoes off
while he paces. "But why did he . . . but what if he . . . I don't
see how . . . ?" Stymied at first, maybe they'll dig deeper,
considering the worn leather dog collar in my bureau,
the scrapbook with missing pages, a photo torn into confetti
then reassembled around certain holes. When I die,
I want these pieces of my life stitched together by a few good
questions, by someone who might finally see that I was
the kind of guy who could stop and smell the roses.
Even at night, even in the passing lane.

Magic Pages

When the world conspires against you, my boy
and one night's worry overshadows a day full of joy

somewhere off the edge of your pillow
a wind still blows through the willows.

There's a secret garden where Winnie the Pooh
shares honey with the old woman in the shoe;

Frog forever wakes Toad, and Peter beats back Hook;
Rikki Tikki Tavi taunts Nagaina in *The Jungle Book.*

There's a place where the wild things still are
and a little prince tells stories about his star,

where the forest of Fangorn grows giving trees
and the Plaza opens its doors to Eloise.

When tomorrow casts shadows like a cage
and yesterday scrawls ink across every page

there's still magic on your shelves, pages allotted.
So much magic, boy. We just grew up, and forgot it.

Truck Stop

Back in my drinking days
we'd eat a late-night breakfast
at the truck stop off I-90,
a back-eddy pool of a 24-hour diner,
the kind of joint that captures a town's
broken and bereft; branches rolling
in froth. Over biscuits and gravy
we sat on cracked plastic seats, kids
playing at being drunks, keeping
one eye on the cautionary tales all
around us, old men sipping coffee
with both hands against the shakes.
Sirens passed outside. One old guy,
unshaven, whispered to his eggs
about vultures, how the vultures had
placed their bets. "My misfortune
means their meal," he mumbled.
"And goddamn ain't that just the way
it goes."

Grandparents

There's little sense
in wondering if
they grieved. They did.
If they hoped. They did.
If they loved. They did.
Oh, they did.
Your grandfather
lay stunned after love
with your grandmother,
stunned and grateful,
and lay touching her face
with wonder and
with gratitude,
the most intimate
of gestures, amazement
that for this moment
he was not so alone.
That they were together,
linked, to bear witness,
to note the progression
of giving, of receiving,
of gratitude and joy.
Thousands of years of it,
a chain of gratitude
stretching back,
grandparent after grandparent.
Think about that.
My god, just think
about it.

On the Yellowstone

My son jumps from rock to rock, from one slick,
half-submerged stone to the next, arms wide,
head tilted in concentration. Some rocks
are perfectly positioned while others come
at a price. He leaps, stretches. We're born knowing
this game, of course, the hopscotch grid,
the cracked sidewalk, and the boy plays it as well
as anyone, keeping his sneakers bone dry,
gradually working his way out into the river.
One slip now and he would be in up to his waist,
or worse. Finally, he stands stymied, islanded away,
teetering above the depths. "I'll come get you,"
I said. I began this poem intending to write
about a certain type of kindness, my wife touching
my shoulder while I sat submerged in a private
backwater of regret and self doubt. Instead, my son
gave me another subject, islanded away, stranded
on his boulder, visibly weighing his options:
the virtues of rescue against the exhilaration
of escape. He could remain where he is or he could
take one more step, plunging down to the bottom
to push off, rushing to the surface, spluttering,
howling, released. It's a coin toss. In this moment,
I can see how it might go either way.
In this moment, his joy.

The View from My Window at Work

A green power box
set on concrete
at an angle; past it,
chain link squaring off
acetylene tanks,
a gnarled crabapple tree,
a field of stubble
not yet filled with houses.
Willows, subdivision,
mountains, a slice of sky,
and all the rest of it.
Odd, how studiously
I inhabit this view
while at my desk and yet
can so easily step away,
taking a leak,
grabbing a soda.
There's everything else
and then there's me.
Among the glorious
mysteries of creation,
I somehow got paid
for writing this poem.
Not to mention
the benefits.

Dandelion Clocks

Time has an appetite
for youth, and devours
slow that which it can't
finish in a bite. Me,
I'm the same guy I was
eight years ago, and yet
every morning I put a plate
of eggs before this boy
who simply somehow
appeared.

The News

You want the good news or the bad news? they say. Me?
I always want the bad news. It's March, the worst month, if you
ask my opinion; though nobody does. Maybe that's the bad news.
There's ice, and the silence that comes during a car crash as your
wheels leave the pavement. But underneath, a subway tremble,
the sounds of life elbowing to the front of the line. Robins stretching
at earthworms and ants pushing sand-grain boulders up their hills.
Birds and dogs always have somewhere better to be. That's the good
news. The way you can lie in the grass and close your eyes against
the sun and hear bees browsing dandelions, winter receding like
a forgotten math test that probably didn't much matter anyway.
I don't believe in God but if I did this would be why:
all the goddamn good news.

Tiny Tragedies

My son brought me a little joy cupped
in his bare hands. "Here," he said.
"I saved this for you, just in case."
We were camping in the Beartooths.
I turned on the propane in a breeze
and kept offering matches to the burner,
again and again, flinching. Every failed
flame was its own tiny tragedy. I found it
hard not to anticipate what comes
next—a flash and smell of singed hair,
a scalding, then the hissing, artificial ring
of heat. We were in the Beartooths.
The worst that can happen, I thought,
is well on its way, and even the best
moments are as fragile and fleeting
as a bird finding your finger. "Give me
your hand," the boy said. "Here's a little
joy."

Quid Pro Quo

The fundamental optimism of history:
We made it till now. The fundamental despair
of the news: brother, there is woe in the world.

I woke this morning to another day busy
inhabiting this particular body tending it,
as I have done, as I will continue to do

for a while, the stew of odors sluiced away
each night, the scrape of a razor around my face,
the cleaning of my teeth. In return, *quid*

pro quo, it will let me trundle along with it for
one more perfectly nice, one more perfectly fine,
one more miraculous little day.

Father's Day

I'm a distasteful man. Can be, anyway.
Profanity is the default. Regret. Self-pity's there
in a pinch. Should have gone to graduate school.
I could have lived in the Dordogne. I envy
the prize winners, the world-weary, the trilingual,
the dry and sophisticated. But this morning,
at the furthest end of every decision, I woke up the boy,
the child who's been dressing himself now for years,
who resists my help, who wakes slow and dislikes
the light, the cessation of warmth, pulling his covers
tight to his chin. In exchange, I'll offer a back scratch,
running my fingernails down the xylophone of his spine,
scratching until the closed eyes are clearly a ruse,
until he starts playing at sleep the longer to keep
the fingernails working. Every choice converges
in this child. To think that it might have been some
other way hobbles me. At 7:15 AM, I find myself
boiled down to essentials. This is me, gone to grit,
reduced to a white rime of gratitude.

Mumblecusser

Hiking with my nine-year-old son last August,
a hot day through cool pines, he turned and said,
"Dadda, did you just say the eff word?" Abashed, caught,
I suppose I did. I know I did. An inadvertent exhalation.
Fuuhhhuck. The boy startling me awake from some
poisonous revery, resentment and regret banging
around inside my head, knocking me out of the present,
away from the chance to watch my son balance, arms wide,
along the imaginary, high-wire edge of the trail; reliving
instead, for the thousandth time, some small slight, some insult,
or maybe thinking about my own misstep, the awful thing
I said, when a word left its barrel to spin toward someone
dear to me, never to be called back. *Asshole,* I mumble.
The word as likely meant for me as otherwise; breathing
it out slow, a whisper, a secret, a luminous sibilant hiss.
Sonofabitch, and man, that satisfies, like chewing a hangnail,
the glory of the profane, the transgressive. *Motherfucker.*
Sometimes it slips out, as inadvertent as a hammer
against a knee, drawing stares in the bookstore, restaurants,
elevators. Am I the only one? I can't be the only one.
How I keep inhabiting the ugliest moments, the landscape
of insults and embarrassments, at the expense
of the gorgeous and elusive now. *Goddamn* but I've got
some work to do. I'm aware. And I'll get to it eventually,
I suppose. But not just yet, not just now. And especially not
these days.

Bastards.

Cordwood

I can't read the news anymore, not this morning at least;
the worst that happened overnight among the billions of us,
and not just the worst—not just emergency rooms and even
funeral parlors, not just adultery from a beloved or a friend's
early heart attack—not just the worst but the unimaginable—
child soldiers slaughtering innocents, outbreaks and explosions,
the dead, as has too often been said, stacked like cordwood.
All of that selected and filtered for the most compelling,
the salacious, that which won't let me look away, that which
won't let me sleep tonight, funneled, sifted carefully through
a screen. Somewhere, for instance, there's a volcano. Fissures
opening, houses igniting like newspapers held over candles,
browning then bursting open into gorgeous flame. I can't
read the news. This morning instead I went to the yard where
we planted trees last weekend—aspens, and an apple tree—
and I unrolled a garden hose and positioned it just so,
just above where the water might do the most good, and I stood
watching it run. From the street, I was another middle-aged dad,
going a little paunchy, aging into his resignation, clutching
at his few accomplishments, maybe trying to remember
what brought him out to the yard in the first place, or maybe
pondering the soil (that was indeed the case) how the roots
were stretching out, slow as scree, as insistent as water finding
the cracks, pushing past earthworms, bacteria, ants, beetles,
the slow, studied frenzy of life under our feet. Somewhere,
thousands of miles from here, a volcano is erupting.
But the real work, the real news, slips past us. Between breaths,
the world somehow, and despite our best apparent efforts,
continues.

Archaeologists

At night the house settles and pops,
a hard wind nudges it along, scrabbling
for purchase. I'm here, awake, clutching
at the mattress, thinking about those
who might eventually excavate
our flattened ruins, the archaeologists
stretching out a grid of string and sticks
then shoveling down toward the beams
of our ceiling, prying up the bricks
of our fireplace, using toothbrushes
to scrape at the scrolled metal of the stove,
finally to photograph, catalogue, sample
the remains of our bed, the linen sheets
charred at the edges, the bones—your femur
thrown over mine, our foreheads touching,
the pebbles of our hands mixed together.
Do you hear it, love? Just there, under
the wind—the scrape of steel
against stone.

The Ice Cutters: A Photo

Two men stand with draft horses
harnessed to a sledge, the sledge filled
with squares of ice, a pale geometry of blue
sawed from the skin of Fort Peck Lake,
harvested to eventually sit in sawdust, shortly
to fill cellars and iceboxes, to keep milk
from spoiling into August. The men stand
dour in the manner of every old photograph,
one in a wool coat and scarf, the other
with his saw. The horses were tamed
by these men, fed hay and oats, harnessed
in a complexity of doubletree, buckles,
chains, leather; the saw sharpened
by these hands, run by the piston push
and pull of their shoulders, fists, elbows.
Ahead of them, a ten-mile trudge up
from the lake on frozen gumbo, deliveries
of ice received and recognized. Did they ask
for the photo to be taken? Did they feel
the rarity of the moment? These men,
their names gone, their stories forgotten;
these men, the saw, the horses, the harnesses,
the ice. I consider what we've lost
and at times it feels like
everything.

The Marmot

snatched up
by the quick
shadow of wings,
trapped within
twin cages of
claws, pierced by
brown needles,
in that final moment
of bloody squeal
and struggle—
Oh man, oh man,
I'm *flying*.

Goodwill

I have far too many shirts in my closet, pressed tight,
crowded shoulder to shoulder, a walk-in reliquary
to off-brand cotton blends and rayons, each shirt
a reminder of mornings spent at the mirror, disheartened
by the soft roll above my belt, buttons straining
to make a break for it; shirts hanging in dim solitude,
in conspiracy with my khakis, threadbare sneakers.
I really need to make a run to Goodwill. All these dress shirts
decades old, dusty on the shoulders, pleated sleeves, raveling
collars, piles of underwear, socks, baseball caps stained
at the brim. Who'd want them? These ghosts of a bygone me,
back when I was fatter, skinnier. I'm not rich unless rich means
having what others don't want. I keep fighting the urge
to apologize. I still haven't made it to Goodwill. Life is accrual
until it becomes loss. Every morning I'm confronted by the failure.
Our job, if you buy the press releases, is to acquire, grab what
you can, race toward the bricks of a predictable epiphany.
Hey, listen: If you don't give it away now it will be taken
from you later. My boy, at some point (fresh from my funeral,
I imagine, grown into an unimaginable adult), will stand
in this closet and consider the army of wrinkled sleeves,
the dress shoes barely worn. The specific odors of his dad.
And this gentle man, fresh from losing his father, running
both hands through his thinning hair, will think: *Christ.*
So I guess maybe Goodwill?

Ranch Trucks

You see them parked behind Quonsets, crooked
on weak springs, bleeding oil into dead grass. Doors dented
by horns and hooves, windshields cracked, a handyman jack
rusted shut. Ford, Chevy, Dodge, they might get three miles
to the gallon if they run at all, fire on five good cylinders
if at all. But they were new once. Fresh off the lot.
Grandchildren rode bareback in their beds, enjoying
the breeze, on their way to building fence, setting posts,
stringing wire loose enough to sway, festooned with
prayer-flag tufts of black hair. Barely containing the cattle
that would soon follow them toward water or grass or only
away from the wind. Pieces of a slow, patient machine,
an engine running on lost fingers, blue thumbnails, drips
of blood and wrenched shoulders. There's wisdom here,
somewhere, grinding slow, turning over. From a back porch,
watching your truck settle down soft into the weeds, here's
a question: How did we ever get so goddamn old?

A Prelude and a Polka

I spent most of the morning
pounding at a poem, tapping time
with my fists, nodding to a beat,
counting feet with my fingers,
going for Gershwin but mostly
getting garbage. Some days
are just better than others.
Today it was all flats and sharps,
hard turns around a tinny
music box, a few measures
to belt out alone at a stoplight.
Fuck it. Even Stravinsky had to start
somewhere. There are all these
heroes who go unsung.
Hey, here's one on the house:
You're not done until you've quit.
You're not beat until you've stopped.
Maybe I'm no Dvořák but
I'm not done, either. You want me,
I'll be over here plinking away,
trying to find a tune big enough
to move your feet.

Piano Lessons

Children, learning piano,
ignore the pauses,
the helpful hesitations
that lend meaning.
They have yet to learn
that it's the silence
on either side of a note
that gives it something
to say. It's a lack of music
that finally makes music.

On a Tree Stand in Montana

In San Francisco and San Diego, Seattle, barges sit
for their cranes; metal arms dip, swing, lift.
Between Oakland and Sacramento, commuters idle
five lanes deep, each car filled with its own private purpose.
Across Texas, oil rigs dip relentlessly. Helicopters hover
over Central Park. This is civilization. What passes for it,
in any case. The frenetic movement of intent across
a neutered landscape. Here in Garfield County, an ant
has been struggling with a crumb from the cracker
I ate shortly after I arrived. Twelve feet away, a muskrat
stitches its way through the water, flipping deep,
then resurfacing again to stitch just as studiously
the other way. An antelope doe and fawn came to water
an hour ago, drinking deeply, fragile-legged and uncertain.
They raised their heads, cautious about coyotes, lions, me.
They haven't been told but they know it in their bones:
Nothing lasts forever.

Meat

We worked in jeans and vests, kneeling
before the swinging carcass, peeling
at our sections of skin, its hair rank
with the smell of wallows and urine,
odors of the rut, slicing skin away
with strategic sweeps of our knives.
We worked in the silence of those
who have done this a hundred times
before, the meat cold from its hanging,
hands cramping. If there is a heaven
it will surely have this. A father and son
working toward a distant meal. Grace.
I hope there is no end to it. I would have it
again and again.

Middle C

All around America, legions
of forgotten pianos, uprights mostly,
loose-toothed and arthritic,
tinny and out of tune, sit waiting
for Mozart, maybe Schubert,
silent in church basements
and rec rooms, impatient
for a set of knotted knuckles
to stumble through "The Entertainer"
or "Amazing Grace," for a toddler
to roll out a series of joyful
glissandos, or for a single
aspiring finger to press middle C,
again and again. Music is always
on its way. Wife, this is a love poem.

Fire Season

Angling into the simmering oven
depths of pine, into the smoky bellows
and angled yellow light of ponderosas,
preceded by a joyous dog, the traffic noise
rises and falls behind me, hissing like surf.
Somewhere in the dry ocean of trees above,
bewildered (I imagine), there's a mule deer
doe, a cow elk, a black bear waiting, all
patiently anticipating my arrival. Are they
aware of the simmering? The ongoing broil
and burn? I want to think no. But I could be
wrong. Hiking, it takes time to leave
the traffic behind, to enter a certain silence,
to leave room for a revelation or even two.
Our grandchildren will say, *You did this to us.*
They will say, *You didn't know how it would be.*
But I tell you now, no. Forgive us. We knew
what we were doing. We just didn't know
how to stop.

The Daily Bones

The day is a piece of art
if you know how to frame it.
Let's talk about grit, the gumption
it takes to slip into a shower,
breakfast, an hour-long commute.
Did you sit briefly on the edge
of the bed, slumped, imagining
another life? Yeah, I know.
Who's got that kind of time.
There's the child's school, laundry.
He needs cleats, underwear,
a dental appointment. Goddamn,
you're a hero, pal, and I hope
you know it. Let's talk bravery,
sacrifices, the courage of bank
accounts waxing and especially waning.
We carry our coffins with us,
of course, though some more lightly
than others. I admit that today
was a trial. Moving furniture
for a friend, I helped lug
a sleeper sofa up narrow stairs.
Afterwards, I stood at the top,
catching my breath, waiting,
waiting for the first wave
of applause.

Yesterday Afternoon, 3:35

Picking up our son from school,
it takes a minute before he sees me
idling in the parking lot.
I don't mind, really. I'm glad
for the pause, for the glimpse
into his life apart from his parents.
Classmates shouting back and forth,
cheerful tussles, heads tucked
under arms, coats pulled
this way and that, a circling tight
around a phone then the flushing
away again, exaggerated
laughter, groans of disbelief.
The boy with his friends, children
considering adulthood but not yet
committed to the purchase.
In the middle, encircled, an audience
of us, the parents listening to NPR,
graying, bemused, texting, tired.
Considering, maybe, other
schoolyards decades removed.
Then one of us calls out a name
and the reverie is broken; children
start to unpiece themselves
from their clusters, pulled each
toward a vehicle. Then the slamming
of car doors, one after another
after another.

Origami

In one of the lives I didn't choose,
I woke early to kindle a fire, to blow flames
up from yesterday's coals, filling a tiny cabin
with the smell of cedar. In another life, I tied
off my dory and limped up to a Cape Cod,
shingles askew, porch peeling paint, carrying
a striper for the grill. In one of the lives
that went on without me, I found a career
in origami, folding paper flowers for tourists.
It's possible, it seems, to build something
beautiful from even the oldest paper bag,
greasy and worn, if you know where to cut,
where to fold, and what to keep.

Man vs. Nature

You'll want to see the
wilderness while you're still young,
tents, campfires, bug dope;

because later, the
wilderness—its howling winds,
a circle of wolves,

vertigo above
the abyss, will be dropping
by your place. You'll need

to know it when it
arrives. The wilderness was
smug the last time I

saw it. "I'm in the
market for a couple good
epiphanies," it said.

Only yesterday
I lay face down in the pine
needles, exhausted.

"Okay fine," I said.
"Fine, goddamnit. You win."

Releasing a Child

It's not sudden. It's not a fish flipping away
from the boat. Rather, it's a tooth extracted
for years. We left the boy in day care to go to work.
Absurd, I thought, that the crude machinery
of the world should tear us so easily apart.
We told ourselves it was probably for the best.
"She seemed nice." Meaning Miss Debbie,
the woman who now held the soft, pudgy knot
of our child's life in her stranger's kind hands, if only
for a few hours three days a week. Years later,
on the first day of kindergarten, he found his name
on a slip of paper propped above an empty desk,
and sat without being asked, tolerating my hug
goodbye, my kiss on the crest of his head where
I'd been watching the hair grow into its cowlick swirl.
We turned from him, and when we waved
from the open door he lifted his hand in return,
but only a little. When he was an infant, parents
would stop at our table and say, "It goes by so fast."
I always hated that. The patronizing wistfulness.
But late last week, leaving a restaurant in a crowd,
there was a young couple with a little boy
in a high chair, six months old, maybe, and before
I could stop myself, I said, so help me I said,
"It all goes by so fast."

Left Behind

In a dim room before my wife wakes,
the wind leaking cold through the door,
under a clicking ceiling fan, before the boy
needs his breakfast, it's just me in my chair,
reading. The life of travel I'd once imagined
has been reduced the way onions in a pan
are reduced. Certain ambitions have smoldered
down to coals. It occurs to me, though,
that the job of an explorer isn't just to travel.
It's also to tell the tale of his travels, to describe
what he saw. Old men fishing with long poles
on slow rivers and sour yellow wine in clay mugs,
brick bridges and cypress-shaded cemeteries.
Those left behind thus have a role to play as well:
to receive the story. I had a dream in which
all those I've lost sat at a campfire, hands open
to the warmth. My grandfather glanced up.
"Take your time, boy," he said, kindly.
"Take all the time you need."

Fistfight

I was in sixth grade and new in town.
A kid tried to pick a fight and I gave it to him;
me with my small fists clenched inside
a circle of cheering twelve-year-olds,
none of whom were cheering for me.
I landed a couple good ones and his nose
began to bleed. He tried not to cry but failed.
They finally rode their bikes away in defeat.
That was a good moment. Worse moments
came later but that one was nice. Later, I accepted
the bullying. Out of fear, I suppose. Not a fear
of being beat up but of something else.
Forty years later, I'm at a loss. What could
have been worse than letting those little turds
diminish me? I've carried it with me for years.
Stand up for yourself, son. I would do it for you
but I can't. Call it the first lesson of adulthood.
When you're twelve and you clench your fists
inside a circle of kids cheering for the other guy,
if you offer him bruises and a bloody nose,
you'll be given back this one beautiful thing:
yourself.

The Photo Album

Were we ever so young?
I was slim and
your mother glowed,
her beauty like you read about.
Son, you trusted us
to give you love, warmth, tickles.
Years ago and just yesterday.
Can our bodies,
our biology handle it?
This blunt evidence
of years gone by?
The days blur, wires spark
between pages
smolder in the spine;
circuits flip,
There's a whiff of ozone.
"Dad, you okay?"
No, it's good. I'm cool.
Until I turn the page
and see once more
how much has been taken
from us. How little
must be left.

The Party

I was the guy who wore collared shirts
to parties in high school, envying
from the edges the effortless cool,
those swaggering few in raveling t-shirts,
threadbare jeans, so thin, so fluid,
so effortlessly self-possessed.
They're gone now, many of them, victims
of cancer, car wrecks, suicide, the debts
called due for every lovely smoke,
every beautiful bottle of booze.
We will die eventually, and forever.
Where was I. Saying something about
empathy. I drove past the Bozeman High
football game last night and the lights
of the field were an island in the dark,
filled with parents cheering, groaning,
laughing, passing along mugs of cocoa,
maybe spiked with booze. And it struck me
as the most heartbreaking thing—
this life lived at the edges.

In Which an Orange Means the World

Chilled from the garage, ripe
from the grocery store, displaced
to my kitchen counter, bought
over my own hesitations (how good
could it be this time of year?),
the orange sat waiting, at once itself
and the potential for itself, sweetness
manifest, grainy and cold. The peel
came apart under my practiced thumbs;
and the sections fell away, discrete
and perfect. I put a few slices on a paper
towel and offered them to the boy.
He declined, distracted by a video game.
"You sure?" I asked. "It's pretty good."
The boy was sure, at least for now.
"Well, it's here," I said, "whenever
you want it."

Fisherman at the Bar

"*This* big, I swear. Took me into my backing
then some. Head on one side of the net,
tail drooping over the other. Salmon fly
a midge in those jaws. The fish would have
its own story but this is mine. How I saw it,
the shape of it, finning dim down deep
among the boulders, the outline, how it rose,
tilting slow and solid toward the surface,
then how I set the hook and let it run before
wrestling it back. The fish would say
it was duped, fooled, jerked away from
the calm meditation of its days only to gasp
in this cruel, alien light. I suppose beauty
depends on whether or not you're the one
holding the rod. I brought the fish to hand,
considered its jaded eye, this slice of river
manifested to muscle, mused on the heartbreak
of a dream realized too soon, then let it slip
back to the depths. The river, the clouds, the fly
floating past; everything we want, everything
we've missed. Friends, you don't go fishing
for the fish.
Still, sumbitch was *this* big."

An Accidental Look in the Mirror

It's the scars
that tell us
who we are.
It's the broken
pieces that
set us apart.
We are all
broken in our
own way. We are
all beautiful
in our broken
way. Like the
world, you are
so broken and
you are so
beautiful.

Forty-Nine Years Old at an Outdoor Bluegrass Concert

Beard going gray, belt cutting into my belly,
I've somewhere picked up a limp and anxiety; our boy
plays in a creek behind the beer garden while my wife
and I stand at a distance, watching younger men and women
crowd the stage, a discrete organism popping with music,
with health, glowing the way heartwood glows under bark,
five hundred arms lifting plastic cups of beer into the sun,
swaying as the mandolin cuts a path, the bass offers a beat,
and clouds of pot smoke roll through steady as exhaust.
Mostly bark now, I'd like to resist the consolations
of judgment: when you're my age, if you only knew
what I know now, one day you'll see. Because honestly,
I'm not sure that I've learned much of anything in the interim.
Age doesn't offer wisdom so much as resignation.
I'm the same guy I always was albeit with a belly, a limp.
But maybe there's more to be said. Take your tribal youth,
your beauty, your mindless joy. Take them. Life is loss
but in the end you'll be left with what you need.
You will be allowed to keep, for a while, everything
that was always anyway the most important. You'll see.
There's no map. You'll know it when
you get there.

An Epiphany

I've been waiting
for a new revelation
to swing at my sails, to
change the scene, to twist
at the horizon, olive trees to
open sea. It's not looking good,
though. We have the same wind
today as yesterday. And as gentle as
it is, as warm as it is, the morning
still plays on repeat: there's just me
and a spray of cold salt water, the
hard sun, complaints from
the gulls, and
me,

waiting

A Political Commentary

Wife rasping gently beside me, I lay
half awake as the earth began to shake.
I grabbed the edge of the mattress. The floor
tilted and span. Our headboard twisted.
Wood splintered and a rumble rose
from the earth, clanking. Odors of tire smoke
and smoldering landfills. Outside, neighbors
took to the street, clutching robes and rifles.
The ground cracked and groaned, split and grinned
wide. I startled awake, uneasy, reassuring
myself, as one does, that it was only a dream.
The earth seemed solid enough, at least for now.
Mumbling to myself (just a dream, Jones,
just a dream) as I went room to room, righting
fallen chairs; straightening paintings newly askew
on their nails, judging their angles. They all
seemed to hang true, if only for now, and if only
by their nails.

The Magic of Middle Age

"It's a puzzle. Why my lawn grows so well but only
in that one little patch. Or how about bruises.
You get those bruises on the shins? And where
did the last week go? For that matter, what about
the last ten years? The people running the show
should be smarter than I am. All this time, I assumed
they knew what they were doing. Joke's on me, I guess.
You come out of your twenties with a plan, not seeing
how the bulk of your life, the armature, will be pounded
up from happenstance. The boards under the Sheetrock
mostly arrange themselves. A coin goes into a fist
and it disappears with a whiff and a kiss. Still, you know
the sonofabitch is around somewhere. What about
those last ten years? Where did those go? I'd like a beer
but shouldn't. I'd like to sleep in, but of course can't.
That'd taste better with salt, but you know, I got
that high blood pressure. The avenues of middle age,
as it turns out, run between cross streets of abstention
and denial. I was forty, and now, just like that—a kiss
and a whiff—I'm fifty. Who knew? I mean,
who the hell knew?"

A Birdwatcher Goes off the Deep End

He preened for
a pretty young
chickadee.
He took a
happy shit
on a humvee.
He burped
the pleasant taste of
honey bees.
He envied the
Robins their nest
in the trees.
He defended
his little piece of
avian sprawl
with a repeating
and most
unpleasant call:
fuckit, fuckit, fuckit
fuckitall.

The Friendship of Men

is hammered together by shared labor, solders
along a common seam, bulwarks against dissolution
and entropy. The friendship of men needs scorn,
derision lacquered over an armature of regard,
it needs a common humor. It's rooted in the shallow soil
of our bodies, older than we feel them to be. It lives
vicariously through the feats of the young—
artful, spiraling passes and balletic end zone leaps.
It thrives before the mistakes of inept coaches
("That guy can't manage a clock. Not at all.") and is hatched
in the nests of elementary schools, angry rounds
of tether ball and world-record swing set jumps.
The friendship of men has a hard time meeting your eyes.
It's susceptible to marriage and alcoholism but
can be revived, briefly, by fishing, a few beers, a game
of pool, a nice compliment. "Helluva shot there."
The friendship of men, shriveled by time and distance,
responds to a strong handshake, a rough half hug.
It's enough that we are here together, you and me,
having called shotgun at just the same moment;
enough that we can sit now shoulder to shoulder,
tight in the front seat, privileged to enjoy the view,
feeling lucky just to have a view.

November Near Huntley, Montana

There's a field of stubble
where the hay used to be,
a scattering of deer pellets,
puddles of clay. Halfway
across the field, I found
a whitetail buck picked clean
by crows, shot from the road
by drunk teenagers, or poachers
who lost their nerve, and left.
Gratitude is a kind of contentment.
Wife, child, family, to imagine
their absence is to clench
and twist, it's to briefly die
before rising again, before
reaching across to touch
a shoulder, a knee, a hand.
Gratitude, it seems, is seeded
in a vision of absence, in drowning
then surfacing again with a gasp.
Walking across a hayfield toward
Pryor Creek, I wrote a poem,
damp at the edges.

Montana: A History

Back then, America stood already askew, tilted
at an alarming angle, then tilted further still
until the loosest lost their grip, the second sons
and daughters from New York, Virginia, the Carolinas,
shavings curled from larger families, the entrenched
and playing-it-safe, the risk-averse, those happy
to release their more adventurous, curious, courageous,
and yes, desperate children, to let them slip
down into the empty map; a wave of immigrants
cruising through the prairie, picking up speed
on the flat, coasting loose until, hitting the mountains,
they said, "Well, ain't this pretty."

And stuck.

The Prince of Highway 200

Let's say you start in Paradise

or Plains, Thompson Falls on the river, the empty, aspiring
boulevards, the dust and grit and asphalt glitter. Point
the headlights east, swerve around some restless shades,
past windows lit by late night sots, early morning insomniacs,
accountants at their coffee pots (dull before the drip, the water clock
diminishment of their days), fry cooks and waitresses unlocking
doors, turning signs, judging coolers and parceling out lunch meats.
The turkey will make it, hopefully,

through the day.

Maybe you have ambitions beyond Paradise, and time enough
to spend on a distant living, the loose change of a distant wage,
even if it means leaving a woman warm in her bed, a child
in his crib, all of you caught in the gears of this particular time,
this particular place. It's in the terms and conditions, spelled out
in the fine print. The town folds itself away behind you. Roads are
arteries, veins, capillaries through the corpus, but this one's gone
varicose, a burst blue bulge, potholes and liver spots.

With me so far?

Buddy, we've seen some things. Kisses blown, fists offered
in anger, skid marks and scars, road signs with bullet holes
("Bet you can't hit the P") the crash and pang, hoot and laugh.
Joy and violence, delight and its aftermath, the various conditions

of the cradle. Maybe try not to take yourself so seriously.
Last February, lost in a blizzard, crawling through the tunnel
of 200 at warp speed—seems like they could have spent more
on the special effects. But this is June by god, the best month;

I'll make a case for it.

End of mud season and whatnot. Preoccupied by memory, lost
in maybe the most beautiful lay you ever had, sunrise takes you
by surprise. It's a symphony now, the road played by long haul
truckers downshifting off tune, strings and winds, the semi
cacophony of horns coming in late, familiar brown vans turning
left, taking their time. The UPS guy could run forever for mayor,
and make it. Where do we belong if not here? Where is home
for us now? A misleading question, maybe misguided.

Maybe I misspoke.

This is when we imitate the sun. Pick at the edges of an idea,
pull it off fast. For now, consider the dead end streets passed at
speed, logging yards gone graveyard quiet, porches peeling scabs
of paint, a camp trailer tilted on three flats. Missoula fades in
the rear view. Consider the bars, the saloons in Bonner, Ovando,
Avon, stools split to show synthetic stuffing, poker
machines casting their reds, greens, blues, all the poisonous hues.
The clap of a window falling shut, a door in the alley banging loose.

I'm not sure anyone's listening.

Bars that used to be banks, bars that used to be beauty salons,
bars with neon signs gone gray, white crosses pounded in threes,
crosses seeded in shots of whiskey and bathtub speed, blooming
thickest on swerves nobody saw coming. Steel crumpling,
glass shattering, then silence, a bone-deep quiet, a gray underbelly
and the tick of dripping antifreeze. We've been lucky so far. Keep it
between the lines and greasy side down. Every cross is draped around
with drunks hipcocked at their ease, bemused,

picking their teeth

from the palms of their hands. Down the length of these borrow pits,
passing bars but churches too, steeples and reader boards spelling out
holy puns, the sweet whiskey burn of self regard smoldering,
congregations drawn into pews to be fed enough fire and brimstone
to make it through the week. Pick your poison, friends. In Moccasin,
sun-baked plastic pumpkins will make sense again come October.
Broken panes in brick buildings of mysterious purpose. I was wrong
before. Not an artery or a vein but a slash, a scar.

Am I making any sense at all?

Most of all, the tilted barns and homestead buildings askew,
sinking into sod. You can tell that somebody tried, families dour
in their only daguerreotype. They did their best. Taking a leak
off the side of the road, there's a trick to timing the traffic. The next
nearest car is still at least five minutes behind. Who'd ever want to live
where you couldn't piss off the side of the road? Don't answer that.
Cemeteries. Home soon whether we like it or not. Domino gravestones
falling forever almost down, containing

all the messy lives

rowed now neat, bookmarked by a pair of years. Highway 200
isn't a scar or a slash so much as a bone, a femur, a backbone splitting
us down the middle, tilting us toward an exit that has, as its only virtue,
expectations for our arrival. Don't forget the hollow spires of grain
elevators, tilted, empty, inhabited by pigeons, mice, hawks, angled bars
of sunlight through dust, the tiny windows played off tune by the wind.
The endlessly unscrolling wind, lips pursed above a beer bottle,
whistling. Not a bone or scar but rather an intestine;

a gut winding through.

The price of gas in Lewistown—eighty bucks for a tank. Christ.
Not the worst news. A u-joint is heading south and a wheel
bearing grinds like cereal under your sole. The Dodge is pushing three
hundred thousand miles and it's got to give up the ghost sometime
soon but not yet, please not yet. What's the point, is a pretty good
goddamn question. Winnett, where a smug deputy once handed
you a ticket, the two of you the only trucks on the road;
Winnett where you went antelope hunting as a boy—

those early reluctant mornings

with the smell of coffee and bacon, a rattletrap RV swaying
behind another unreliable Dodge; a child in the company of men,
small shoulders squeezed into a front seat, three rifles barrel
down between knees, a .30-06, a .243, a 7mm, the smell of smokes
and bodies, last night's whiskey stewing in stale sweat; years later,
jacklighting, teenagers twisting a spotlight out the window, beers
between the legs, freezing fingers off for just one glimpse of a pair
of glowing green eyes beside the berm.

It never made much sense, I admit.

We've all been wrung dry, twisted tight for every last dollar.
There's a conspiracy at hand. Tell me, pal, where do I surrender?
Or rather, should we stop for a drink? Even knowing where it might lead.
Get the timing right, Sidney might have a stool that fits your rump.
A beer sounds good. A beer and a bump. In North Dakota, just over the
border, the pumps are at it even now, novelty desktop birds dipping beaks,
wells flaring off, lighting each their claim, mine and mine
but not by god yours. Not yours.

Let's say you arrive.

Two hundred isn't an artery or a vein, not a bone but rather a bank.
A cool blue evening and cows bundled in the berm, a prairie filled
with fiberboard and house wrap, nail guns tapping a common time. What
have we lost and what have we gained? It's above my pay grade. Tire tread
traded for a view, golden eagles running sheep, coyotes casing
the place, ravens flaring up from a roadkill ribcage. Buddy, see,
here's the thing: We thought we were leaving home. But no.
We were misled. All this time,

home's been leaving us instead.

Afterword

First poem to last, this collection spans nearly twenty years. The oldest poem was written in my early thirties, the most recent was printed out last week. It's been an unexpected opportunity, compiling the collection, stacking them all together like this, letting them rub up against each other. At a certain distance, you can reassess, revisit, take a fresh look, recognize the connective tissue, put a name to the themes.

These poems, as far as I can tell now, are about late-life fatherhood, about aging and mortality, they're about trying to see clearly. They're about trying to discover what I think. They're exercises in self-pity and self-absorption. They are coins tossed off the back of a train. They are the 4:00 AM rants of an insomniac and they are the prissy, curated bonsai trees of a pompous little nitpicker. They're doorstops you trip over and Rorschach oil spills you slide across. Most of all, though, they're the rubberized ceiling straps you grab onto when the bus lurches away from the curb.

It's not for me to say if they're any good. What I *will* say, though, is that they aspire to be part of a continuum, part of a tradition.

Cynthia Ozick wrote, "You cannot have Philip Roth without Franz Kafka; you cannot have Kafka without Joseph the dreamer. You cannot have William Gass without Walter Pater; you cannot have Pater without Pindar." Amen, and take it to the bank. For me, those names are Jack Gilbert and Jim Harrison, Mary Oliver and Czeslaw Milosz, Alan Dugan and Seamus Heaney, Ted Kooser and William Stafford, Carolyn Forché and Raymond Carver, also, Bishop and Yeats, Whitman, and Stevens . . . all the deities. When it comes to poetry, I'm no aesthete. I like what I like, and sometimes Mad Dog tastes just as fine as Médoc. But I would be remiss if I didn't acknowledge my debts.

The other thing I want to mention: The amount of effort it takes to grind and polish and ultimately release a poem is all out of keeping with the paycheck. There is no paycheck. And this is, I believe—counterintuitively, perhaps—one of poetry's foundational virtues, particularly in America. It remains largely unpolluted by commerce. Freed of the need to find a buyer, to pander to the marketplace, a poem has a decent shot at being, well . . . decent. A more or less accurate reflection of the writer's aesthetic and associational sensibilities. *Art.* Quality should be poetry's only qualifier. Does a poem *move* me?

This also partly explains why most of these poems have gone unpublished until now. I haven't *tried* to publish. I've been cautious about presenting them to the marketplace (such as it is), offering them up for acceptance or rejection. In that context, I am grateful to Editor Scott McMillion who accepted "The Prince of Highway 200" for publication in *Montana Quarterly* even as this book was going to press. A huge thank you as well to artist Dale Livezey for contributing the extraordinary image used on this cover. Finally, I owe an enormous debt to the Drumlummon Institute and Executive Director Aaron Parrett for agreeing to publish the original, hardcover edition of *Mumblecusser.* I can't begin to express how much Drumlummon's support means to me.

Charles Simic wrote, "The secret wish of poetry is to stop time. The poet wants to retrieve a face, a mood, a cloud in the sky, a tree in the wind, and take a mental photograph of that moment in which you as a reader recognize yourself. Poems are other people's snapshots in which we recognize ourselves."

I love this, and think about it often. And implicit within Simic's conceit, consider the importance of a readership. In order for the cycle of a poem's creation to be complete, there needs to be an audience at the end, at least one reader waiting to receive it, someone who might ideally recognize aspects of their own life between the lines. A poem that goes unread is no poem at all.

Thank you, dear reader, for flipping through these snapshots.

About the Author

He's maybe not the sharpest tool
in the shed, the brightest bulb
in the pack. It's been a solid year
since he slept through the night,
longer since he took a good hard look
in the mirror. There are those who
appear to understand calculus,
who take a better author photo,
who have the wise and world-weary,
self-effacing bemusement down pat.
There are those who seem to be
pleased with their weight, who don't
limp under the burden of their own
bruised expectations. But friends,
for better or worse, take it or leave it,
there is no one, no one else, who
might have written these, these, *these*
goddamn poems.

www.ingramcontent.com/pod-product-compliance
Lightning Source LLC
Chambersburg PA
CBHW030933250426
43631CB00005B/21
* 9 7 8 0 9 9 6 1 5 6 0 5 9 *